21st Century Skills INNOVATION *Library*

Baseball

by Michael Teitelbaum

INNOVATION IN SPORTS

Published in the United States of America by Cherry Lake Publishing
Ann Arbor, Michigan
www.cherrylakepublishing.com

Content Adviser: Thomas Sawyer, EdD, Professor of Recreation and Sport Management, Indiana
State University

Photo Credits: Cover and page 1, ©iStockphoto.com/padnpen; page 5, ©RCPPHOTO, used under
license from Shutterstock, Inc.; page 7, ©afaizal, used under license from Shutterstock, Inc.; pages 8
and 26, ©AP Photo; page 11, ©iStockphoto.com/fredrocko; page 12, ©Todd S. Holder, used under
license from Shutterstock, Inc.; page 15, ©Richard Paul Kane, used under license from Shutterstock,
Inc.; page 17, ©Scott L. Williams, used under license from Shutterstock, Inc.; page 18, ©iStockphoto.
com/ RBFried; page 21, ©AP Photo/David J. Phillip; page 22, ©Plus One Pix/Alamy; page 25,
©AP Photo/National Baseball Hall of Fame; page 27 ©Chad McDermott, used under license from
Shutterstock, Inc.; page 28, ©AP Photo/stf

Library of Congress Cataloging-in-Publication Data
Teitelbaum, Michael.
 Baseball / by Michael Teitelbaum.
   p. cm.–(Innovation in sports)
 Includes index.
 ISBN-13: 978-1-60279-255-5
 ISBN-10: 1-60279-255-0
 1. Baseball–Juvenile literature. 2. Baseball–United
States–History–Juvenile literature. I. Title. II. Series.
 GV867.5.T448 2009
 796.357–dc22   2008002310

Cherry Lake Publishing would like to acknowledge the work of
The Partnership for 21st Century Skills.
Please visit www.21stcenturyskills.org for more information.

CONTENTS

INNOVATION IN SPORTS

CHAPTER ONE

Play Ball!

There are many theories about the beginnings of baseball. According to one story, in 1839, a man named Abner Doubleday invented baseball in the **rural** town of Cooperstown, New York. Playing a game known as town ball in a cow pasture, Doubleday grew tired of the game's loose rules. Every ball was fair. There weren't set paths between bases. This caused **rival** players or even teammates to crash into each other while chasing the batted ball.

And so Abner Doubleday laid out a diamond shape in that cow pasture. He set up baselines and fair and foul territory. And he helped create the game now known as baseball.

This story, however, is not true. For many years people believed it, but it is just a legend.

Baseball is just one of a number of games in which players use bats and balls.

Baseball wasn't really born in small-town America. It began in New York City. On September 23, 1845, a young man named Alexander Joy Cartwright wrote a list of rules for what would become the game we now call baseball.

Games using bats and balls have been played for thousands of years. Ancient Egyptian, European, and Native American cultures had such games. But baseball as it is played today evolved mainly from two British games—cricket and rounders.

These two games were brought to America by the British colonists. They evolved into various bat-and-ball games played in different parts of the colonies. Alexander Cartwright and his teammates in New York played one variation called base ball. This two-word name would eventually become one word and develop into the sport we know today.

Cartwright's 28-man team was called the New York Knickerbocker Base Ball Club. They played **pick-up games** against each other in a beautiful park called the Elysian Fields. There, on June 19, 1846, the first official baseball game was played between two different teams using Cartwright's new rules.

Over the next decade, many more teams were formed. In 1857, the Knickerbockers and approximately 20 other teams that now played by the new rules formed the first baseball league. It was called the National Association of Base Ball Players. By the mid-1860s, many more teams had joined this association. The organization required that all players be **amateurs**. But this would soon change.

Cricket is another game that is played with a bat and ball.

In about 1867, a former cricket player and member of Cartwright's Knickerbocker team named Harry Wright moved to Cincinnati. Led by the Cincinnati Buckeyes, baseball had become popular in that city. Already, some players were secretly being paid to play. Or they would be paid to work jobs that in fact involved little, if any, actual work.

The Boston Pilgrims and Pittsburgh Pirates played in the first World Series at the Huntington Avenue Baseball Grounds in Boston, Massachusetts, in 1903.

Harry Wright decided to openly offer salaries to the best baseball players he could find. By 1869, he had signed nine players for his new team, the Cincinnati Red Stockings. Baseball's first professional team was born. The team still plays today, known simply as the Cincinnati Reds.

Wright knew that to pay his players, he'd have to charge people to watch their games. He figured that if people were willing to pay 75 cents to $1.50 to see a play, many would pay 25 to 50 cents to watch a baseball game. He was right. He was the first to believe that people would pay to see baseball. The sport just had to feature talented, quality players who promised an exciting game. Wright saw baseball as a business.

21st Century Content

America's national pastime is also a global sport. Baseball is played in countries all over the world, from Japan to Mexico. There are now more international players playing in the major leagues than at any time in the game's history. More than 20 nations are represented in the majors today.

In 1871, a new league called the National Association of Professional Base Ball Players was formed. This organization was replaced in 1876 by the National League of Professional Base Ball Clubs. This new league would soon come to be called the National League.

The popularity of professional baseball took off. In 1901, the American League was formed. It remains the National League's rival to this day. In 1903, the two leagues agreed to play a World's Championship Series, or World Series as it came to be known. An American sports institution was born.

Since that time, new teams have been added to each league through **expansion**. And thousands of players have thrilled the paying public.

Rules and Strategy

The game that Alexander Cartwright **standardized** in 1845 was a wild and dangerous affair. Before he came along, baseball was in need of some clear, structured rules. For example, any ball that was hit was in play and had to be chased down, no matter where it went. Cartwright established foul lines. These lines marked the parts of the field where the ball was and wasn't in play.

Cartwright changed the layout to the shape of a diamond. The four bases were each 90 feet (27.4 meters) apart. Bases of a set size replaced sticks and rocks. These changes assured that every game was played under the same field conditions.

Teams were made up of nine players. Three played in the outfield. Cartwright added a new position in the infield called the shortstop. He also established a batting

Alexander Cartwright changed the layout of the baseball field to the familiar diamond shape still used today.

order. This is the order that players come up to bat. It had to remain constant throughout the game.

Each batter now was allowed three missed swings before being called out. Only three batters, rather than the entire team, had to be called out to end an inning. This made the scoring of runs more difficult. Pitchers were required to throw underhand. An umpire was brought in to settle arguments. Teams also began wearing uniforms.

A fielder reaches to tag a runner out during a Little League baseball game.

But the biggest innovation Cartwright put into place had to do with how runners were thrown out. A fielder used to have to throw the ball at the runner and hit him with the ball to get him out. Under the new rules, runners were either tagged out or the ball was thrown to a fielder at a base. That fielder would then step on the base to get the runner out.

Once Cartwright had set up formal rules, the game began to grow in popularity. The person most responsible for helping it grow was Henry Chadwick. Chadwick was a British-born **journalist**. After seeing a game in 1856, he fell in love with baseball and began writing about the sport.

Chadwick convinced the *New York Times* (and later, other newspapers) to publish baseball results. He became the country's first baseball writer and editor. He created the newspaper box score, still used today, which measures each player's performance against the others. Baseball's obsession with **statistics**, a huge part of any fan's appreciation for the game, began with Henry Chadwick.

The rules continued to evolve. To speed up the game, the concept of balls and strikes was added in the early 1860s. The role of pitchers began to change, too. Pitchers no longer simply threw the ball to the batter. They began trying to prevent him from hitting the ball.

During that decade, a pitcher named Candy Cummings threw the first curveball. This new pitch totally **mystified** batters. By the 1880s, this pitch had become more popular. Harry Wright came up with the idea of changing the speed at which pitchers threw.

He also invented the **changeup**. Now pitchers were suddenly mixing up their pitches to fool batters. And so began baseball's ongoing struggle between offense and defense.

In baseball's first years, the game was all about scoring runs. Now with these pitching innovations, the pitchers began to dominate. To even things out, the pitcher was moved further away from home plate. This change made it harder to get batters out.

Under Cartwright's rules, the pitcher stood 45 feet (13.7 m) from home plate. In 1881, this distance was changed to 50 feet (15.2 m). Then in 1893, it was changed again to its current distance of 60 feet 6 inches (18.4 m).

In the early days of baseball, there was no pitcher's mound. The pitcher stood on flat ground. In the early 1900s, a mound was added to give the pitcher an advantage. It was 15 inches (38.1 centimeters) high. This was lowered to the current height of 10 inches (25.4 cm) in 1969. This lower height led to more offense.

Pitchers are often weak hitters. So in 1973, the American League introduced the designated hitter. This player bats in place of the pitcher and does not play a field position.

Some aspects of baseball evolved simply because there were no rules against them. In 1863, a player named Ned

Today's pitchers stand on a mound. They have a greater advantage over hitters than pitchers in baseball's early days who threw from flat ground.

Cuthbert ran from first to second base before the pitcher threw his pitch. Cuthbert pointed out to the umpire that there was no rule against what he had just done. And so, the stolen base was born.

Life & Career Skills

Since 1939, children in the United States have played Little League baseball. These organized teams and leagues are a training ground for young players to learn baseball skills. They teach valuable lessons in teamwork, respect for others, and responsibility.

How do you think baseball and other team sports teach these lessons?

The 1894 Baltimore Orioles added some major **strategic** innovations to the game. They introduced the idea of moving defensive players to the left or right depending on the strength of individual hitters. This is known as shading. They also invented sets of signals so that players on a team could communicate with one another.

The use of speed and stolen bases dominated the game in the first two decades of the 1900s. During those years, Ty Cobb was the game's first superstar base stealer.

But the game changed again in the 1920s with the arrival of Babe Ruth. He began hitting more home runs in a season than some entire teams. The age of the great power hitter had begun.

Jackie Robinson's arrival in 1947 brought back speed and the stolen base. This African American player is best known as the man who broke baseball's color barrier.

CHAPTER THREE

Equipment

Bat, ball, and glove. These are the three essential pieces of equipment for any baseball game. Would you believe that when the game began in 1845, players didn't wear gloves? If you needed a glove, then you weren't tough enough for baseball!

The first baseball gloves appeared in the mid-1870s. They were thin pieces of leather with no padding and no fingers. They provided only a little protection to the

Today's baseball gloves have separate fingers and thick padding.

Catchers haven't always worn the protective gear we are familiar with today.

fielder's palm. When star player Albert Spalding started wearing a glove, other players figured that it was okay. In time, more and more players began wearing them. They realized that gloves might help prevent injuries to their hands. By the 1890s, fingers and padding were added and gloves were more acceptable.

Over the decades, gloves were **customized** for various field position. Catcher's mitts were given extra padding for protection from fastballs. An outfielder's glove had long, deep pockets to help snag fly balls.

Catchers used to play without protective equipment. Then overhand pitching came along in the 1880s. Balls began arriving at home plate with much greater speed. This could be dangerous! By the beginning of the 1900s, face masks, chest protectors, and shin guards had become commonplace. Changes in the rules led to these changes in equipment. Today, catcher's masks resemble the helmets that hockey goalies wear. They offer more protection than ever.

Pitchers have always thrown inside, close to the plate, trying to keep batters off-balance. In 1920, a player named Ray Chapman was hit in the head by a pitch and later died. Talk of adding a hard helmet to protect batters began. But nothing was done for many years.

The Brooklyn Dodgers began wearing plastic inserts inside their baseball caps in the 1940s. By 1952, the Pittsburgh Pirates began wearing batting helmets made of hard plastic. They were similar to the ones in use today. The American League began using helmets in the 1950s. It wasn't until 1971 that Major League Baseball finally made it **mandatory** for all players to wear helmets at the plate.

Life & Career Skills

Sometimes a baseball team may look like nine individuals running in nine different directions. But teams win when they play as a unit. Communication is essential. The catcher flashes signs to the pitcher so they both know what type of pitch he is about to throw. One outfielder backs up another in case the ball gets past the first one. A good team works productively together. They share a common goal: winning the game.

Players were still getting hit on the head just below the helmet, though. So in 1983, it was required that all batting helmets have earflaps on the side that faced the pitcher.

One major innovation in baseball had nothing to do with gloves, bats, balls, or protective equipment. The change was to the playing surface. Beginning with the construction of the Houston Astrodome in 1965, artificial turf began replacing real grass in new stadiums.

Why did the owners choose artificial turf? This fake grass was cheaper in the long run and required much less maintenance. It also allowed domes to be built onto stadiums. Now games could be played in all kinds of weather. With artificial turf, no sun or water was needed.

But new doesn't necessarily mean better. Players suffered more injuries playing on artificial turf, and it became less popular. Today, new stadiums are once again equipped with natural grass.

CHAPTER FOUR

Training

Today, baseball players earn multimillion-dollar salaries. So it is hard to imagine that, in the past, players had to work second jobs in the off-season. They had little time left for fitness training.

Today's baseball players are supreme athletes. They train all year. Many work with fitness coaches and personal trainers. They use the latest in cardio and strength-building equipment. Today's players also follow a strict routine to keep themselves in shape.

Baseball players spend hours stretching, training, and conditioning.

Innovations in technology have also led to advances in how players practice the individual skills of the game. Branch Rickey was one of baseball's greatest innovators. He introduced mechanical pitching machines and batting

Branch Rickey introduced pitching machines.
Today, many coaches use them.

cages for training. This allowed batters to practice hitting without a pitcher or a catcher.

Imagine being able to examine your own performance on the field. The arrival of videotape in the 1960s allowed players to do just that. They could watch themselves after the game to evaluate their moves at the plate. Teams could also watch tapes of pitchers they were going to face. That way, they could study their technique.

Today, a player can open a laptop in the dugout during a game. He can then study what he just did right or wrong at bat or on the field. This innovation allows players to make adjustments during the course of a game.

21st Century Content

Some of baseball's best players were not the healthiest. Babe Ruth, perhaps the greatest player of all time, was out of shape. He had a big belly and often went out for a huge steak dinner after a game. Mickey Mantle, the top home run hitter of his time, went out drinking to celebrate a victory.

Today, athletes follow strict training routines. They work at building strength, flexibility, and endurance. They watch their diet and eat foods that help them stay in top shape. They know that a long, successful athletic career depends on taking steps to ensure lasting health and to prevent injury.

Some Famous Innovators

Henry Chadwick

Henry Chadwick is sometimes called the Father of Baseball. He was one of the sport's most innovative forces in the 19th century. Chadwick helped introduce baseball to the public. He was the first sportswriter to cover baseball. He also invented the box score. This statistical summary of a game was easily reviewed by fans in newspapers.

He pioneered the idea of keeping track of a player's achievements through statistics. This enabled fans and players alike to compare one player's performance to another. He pioneered the idea of a hitter's batting average and a pitcher's earned run average. These are still used as the main measures of a player's ability.

HENRY CHADWICK

BASEBALL'S PREEMINENT PIONEER
WRITER FOR HALF A CENTURY.
INVENTOR OF THE BOX SCORE.
AUTHOR OF THE FIRST RULE-BOOK
IN 1858. CHAIRMAN OF RULES
COMMITTEE IN FIRST NATION-WIDE
BASEBALL ORGANIZATION.

Henry Chadwick was one of the greatest sportswriters of all time.

Chadwick published the first history of the game. He was the first to envision the sport as America's national game. This dream eventually came true.

Babe Ruth was baseball's first great power hitter.

Babe Ruth

During the 1919 Black Sox scandal, it was proven that players lost the World Series on purpose. Fans were outraged, and the survival of baseball was very much in doubt.

Enter George Herman "Babe" Ruth. Speed and pitching had dominated the game for the previous 20 years. In 1919, the "Babe" hit a record 29 home runs.

The following year, he hit an astounding 54—more than most teams. The era of the home run had arrived. Ruth was an innovator because he changed the nature of the game. To this day, the home run remains the dominant offensive play in the game. Babe helped fans forget the scandal and reenergized their love for the game.

Today, many professional baseball players begin their careers playing on minor league teams.

Branch Rickey

Branch Rickey was the most influential person in baseball in the 20th century.

His first major innovation was the creation of the minor league farm system to develop young talent. Before Rickey, minor league teams all operated independently. In the 1920s, as general manager of the St. Louis Cardinals, he began buying minor league teams. He made them all part of the Cardinals organization. He saw the potential of the farm system. It allowed the major league Cardinals to scout and develop players who would

Branch Rickey talks to Dodgers players (from left) Gil Hodges, Gene Hermanski, and Jackie Robinson in 1949.

eventually play for them. They could select the best players of the bunch. This innovation paid off. From 1926 to 1934, the Cardinals won five pennants.

Rickey opened the first full-time spring training facility. He also pioneered the use of batting cages and pitching machines. Many believe he was the first general manager to insist players wear batting helmets.

But Rickey's biggest contribution to the game came when he was general manager of the Brooklyn Dodgers. In 1947, he brought Jackie Robinson to the team. Robinson was the first African American player in the major leagues in more than 60 years. This opened the door for the many great African American players that followed. It also was an early step in the young and growing civil rights movement in the United States.

Learning & Innovation Skills

When Branch Rickey brought Jackie Robinson into the major leagues, both men knew that the road ahead would not be a smooth one. Robinson would face tremendous racism from the crowd, his opponents, and even some of his own teammates.

Rickey explained to the young player that he would need to keep his cool and not lose his temper. To work effectively with his teammates, Robinson would have to be patient. That would mean not responding to insults. As Robinson sat in Rickey's office, Rickey taunted him with terrible racial slurs. He tried to show Robinson what he would face as a player. Rickey wanted a player with the courage to not fight back. Robinson agreed and went on to make history.

Do you think that you would have had the courage to not fight back if you had been in Jackie Robinson's position?

Glossary

amateurs (AM-uh-churz) people who do something without getting paid for doing it

changeup (CHANG-up) a slow pitch thrown with the same motion as a fastball to deceive the batter

customized (KUHSS-tuh-mized) made for a very specific purpose

expansion (ek-SPAN-shuhn) the process of growing or adding to

journalist (JUR-nuhl-ist) a writer or reporter of news

mandatory (MAN-duh-tor-ee) must be done

mystified (MISS-tuh-fide) confused

pick-up games (PIK-up GAYMZ) informal games played among friends

rival (RYE-vuhl) competing

rural (RUHR-uhl) out in the country

standardized (STAN-durd-eyezd) made uniform or even

statistics (stuh-TISS-tiks) numbers used to measure or compare things

strategic (struh-TEE-jik) carefully planned in order to win or achieve a goal

For More Information

BOOKS

Fleder, Rob, ed. *Sports Illustrated: The Baseball Book*. New York: Time Inc. Home Entertainment, 2006.

Jacobs, Greg. *The Everything Kids' Baseball Book: Today's Superstars, Great Teams, Legends—and Tips on Playing Like a Pro*. Avon, MA: Adams Media, 2006.

Lipsyte, Robert. *Heroes of Baseball: The Men Who Made It America's Favorite Game*. New York: Atheneum, 2005.

WEB SITES

Baseball Almanac
www.baseball-almanac.com/
An excellent source for player bios, stats, and info on the game's history

Baseball Timeline
www.pbs.org/kenburns/baseball/timeline/
A timeline of key events in baseball history

The Official Site of Major League Baseball
http://mlb.mlb.com/index.jsp
Find statistics and info on players past and present

Index

About the Author

Michael Teitelbaum has been a writer and editor of children's books and magazines for more than 25 years. His fiction features characters ranging from Garfield to Spider-Man. His latest work of fiction is *The Scary States of America*, published by Delacorte in 2007. His most recent nonfiction books include *Mountain Biking*, *Rock Climbing*, and *Skiing* for Cherry Lake Publishing. He and his wife, Sheleigh, live in New York City.